CLASSIC
StoryTellers

JOHN STEINBECK

Mitchell Lane
PUBLISHERS

P.O. Box 196
Hockessin, Delaware 19707

Titles in the Series

C L A S S I C
Story Tellers

JOHN STEINBECK

by Kathleen Tracy

Copyright © 2005 by Mitchell Lane Publishers, Inc. All rights reserved. No part of this book may be reproduced without written permission from the publisher. Printed and bound in the United States of America.

Printing 1   2   3   4   5   6   7   8
Library of Congress Cataloging-in-Publication Data

Tracy, Kathleen.
    John Steinbeck / Kathleen Tracy.
        p. cm. — (Classic Storytellers)
    Includes bibliographical references and index.
    Contents: An eye for detail — Surrounded by nature — Breaking through — Giving workers a voice — A literary legacy.
    ISBN 1-58415-271-0 (lib. bdg.)
        1. Steinbeck, John, 1902-1968 — Juvenile literature. 2. Novelists, American — 20th century — Biography — Juvenile literature. [1. Steinbeck, John, 1902-1968. 2. Authors, American. 3. Nobel Prizes — Biography. 4. Authorship.] I. Title. II. Series.
    PS3537.T3234Z929 2004
    813'.52—dc22
                                                                                              2003024139

ABOUT THE AUTHOR: Kathleen Tracy has been a journalist for over twenty years. Her writing has been featured in magazines including The Toronto Star's "Star Week," *A&E Biography* magazine, *KidScreen* and *TV Times*. She is also the author of numerous biographies including "The Boy Who Would be King" (Dutton), "Jerry Seinfeld - The Entire Domain" (Carol Publishing), "Don Imus - America's Cowboy" (Carroll & Graf), "Mariano Guadalupe Vallejo," and "William Hewlett: Pioneer of the Computer Age," both for Mitchell Lane. She recently completed "Diana Rigg: The Biography" for Benbella Books.

PHOTO CREDITS: Cover, pp. 1, 3, 20 Getty Images; p. 6 Corbis; p. 15 Mrs. E. G. Ainsworth, Courtesy of the Steinbeck Archives of the Salinas Public Library, Salinas, California; p. 25 Steinbeck Research Center, San Jose State University; p. 26 Getty Images; p. 31 Dorothea Lange; pp. 34 Corbis.

PUBLISHER'S NOTE: This story is based on the author's extensive research, which she believes to be accurate. Documentation of such research is contained on page 45.

The internet sites referenced herein were active as of the publication date. Due to the fleeting nature of some web sites, we cannot guarantee they will all be active when you are reading this book.

Contents

JOHN STEINBECK
by Kathleen Tracy

*For Your Information

In his later years, John Steinbeck, and his third wife, Elaine, made their home in Sag Harbor, New York. But Steinbeck will always be most closely associated with his childhood home in California's Salinas Valley. His best known books, *The Grapes of Wrath* and *Of Mice and Men*, are set among the migrant work camps of Central California. Those books brought to light the migrant workers' plight of poverty and hopelessness.

Chapter 1

AN EYE FOR DETAIL

Many authors write books about fantastic creatures or magical worlds they imagine in their own minds. John Steinbeck was different. He preferred to use real people and real places as his inspiration. He thought of himself more as a journalist than as an author.

To bring the characters who populated his books to life, Steinbeck would study people around him and absorb their characteristics, their lifestyles and their idiosyncrasies, or their unique traits. He spent countless hours walking through towns such as Monterey and Salinas along California's central coast, or staying in migrant workers' camps. He memorized sights, sounds, colors and even smells so he'd be able to recreate them later on paper.

That attention to detail became second nature for Steinbeck. Years later his son, Thom Steinbeck, said that his father's knack for re-creating the language and life of the places he wrote about was the result of an endless curiosity. Sometimes that endless curiosity got annoying for his family.

"My father once gave me this thing called The Big Ear, a plastic toy you'd use to hear things far away," Thom recalled. "Well, he stole it back from me. In restaurants he'd pay more attention to conversations at other tables than at ours."[1]

When Steinbeck was 27, America was plunged into the Great Depression. He continued to listen to people. He also began to care about the hardships he saw around him. The area hardest hit during the Depression was the Great Plains states, which suffered a severe seven-year drought beginning in 1931. When a series of dust storms hit the region a year later, many farms literally dried up and blew away in the wind. The devastation was so enormous that about 150,000 square miles of land in the southern Great Plains came to be called the Dust Bowl. The disaster left hundreds of thousands of farmers and their families homeless and with no means of support.

Many of those who lost their land made their way to California. The state's fertile central valley and warm climate enabled farmers there to grow many types of produce. By the time the Depression began, California was already a world leader in agriculture. Because the growing season lasted all year long, there was always the need for migrant farm workers to pick and harvest the crops. Despite horrible living conditions, these desperate families came by the thousands.

Steinbeck was curious about who these migrant workers were. He traveled among them, observing and absorbing their lives. The suffering, low pay and unsanitary conditions he saw profoundly affected him, both personally and professionally. He would later use their stories as inspiration for many of his novels.

In those novels, he demonstrated his ability to make his readers feel as if they were right with the characters. His special skill was bringing his characters to life in a way that was both entertaining and showing social awareness. This ability eventually earned him the world's greatest honor for an author: the Nobel Prize for Literature. According to the Nobel Prize committee, the reason for the award was "his realistic and imaginative writings, combining as they do sympathetic humor and keen social perception."[2]

In his acceptance speech, Steinbeck talked about what he thought it meant to be a writer. "The ancient commission of the writer has not changed," he said. "He is charged with exposing our many grievous faults and failures, with dredging up to the light our dark and dangerous dreams for the purpose of improvement."[3]

In the same speech, he also talked about the importance of literature to any civilization. It allows us to not only see ourselves, but also those we may not otherwise think about or be aware of.

"Literature is as old as speech," he explained. "It grew out of human need for it and it has not changed except to become more needed...Writers are not separate and exclusive. From the beginning, their functions, their duties, their responsibilities have been decreed by our species...the writer is delegated to declare and to celebrate man's proven capacity for greatness of heart and spirit–for gallantry in defeat, for courage, compassion and love. In the endless war against weakness and despair, these are the bright rally flags of hope...I hold that a writer who does not passionately believe in the perfectibility of man has no dedication nor any membership in literature."[4]

Chapter 1 AN EYE FOR DETAIL

Steinbeck spent much of his life writing about people's courage in the face of adversity. His own life reads more like a story of high adventure. He was born with a spirit of wanderlust, or a desire not to stay too long in any one place. California, with its spacious natural beauty and diverse population, would prove the perfect place for him to grow up.

FYInfo

Roaring Twenties

Ford's Model T

While the Great Depression was undoubtedly economically disastrous, it also dealt Americans a crushing emotional blow because it came on the heels of what many people considered a Golden Age in the United States.

After the turn of the twentieth century, Americans were riding a wave of unprecedented personal prosperity and economic success. The industrial revolution had made the United States the richest country on earth and it seemed the good times would never end. People spent money as fast as they earned it – and in many cases, *before* they earned it. Credit and loans were easy to obtain and people happily lined up to benefit from the banks' largesse, or excessive generosity. People were blinded by optimism, preferring not to see the dangers lurking ahead.

The decade of the 1920s in particular epitomized the high-flying life-style. Dubbed the "Roaring Twenties," it was a time of flappers, women getting the right to vote and entering the work force, Ford's Model-T making cars affordable to the average consumer, job security, the first transatlantic airplane flight, and the rise of the movies. In many ways, it was similar to the 1960s because America was undergoing a major social evolution and revolution.

Some people warned that the good times couldn't last forever. But there didn't seem to be any need to worry about the future. Most Americans were able to support themselves comfortably and were able to borrow whatever money they needed to buy a car or some other modern convenience. By the end of the decade, people began to find themselves buried in debt and unable to keep up payments. Unemployment began to rise and as people ran out of money to spend, industrial production drastically declined, causing more jobs to be lost. Worst of all, stock market prices were inflated, meaning people spent more on stock than it was worth.

On October 29, 1929, the stock market crashed, leaving thousands penniless overnight. In one dramatic day, the Roaring Twenties came to a stunning, catastrophic end as the Great Depression soon locked America in its grip.

California's Salinas Valley is known as "The Salad Bowl of the World." It is the world's premiere produce supplier. In order to harvest all the crops that are grown, landowners employ migrant workers. As a young man, Steinbeck traveled with these workers and these experiences would change his life.

Chapter 2

SURROUNDED BY NATURE

For the young John Steinbeck, Central California was more than just where he lived. It was part of who he was. Born on February 27, 1902, he grew up in the Salinas Valley, an agricultural community of incredibly fertile soil. It is nicknamed "The Salad Bowl of the World" because of all the produce grown there. The Salinas River is the largest submerged stream in the nation, and its underground waters provide irrigation for the valley's fields. Located about a hundred miles south of San Francisco, Salinas was settled shortly after the Gold Rush of 1849. With the arrival of the Southern Pacific Railroad in 1872, it quickly became the major trading center for the region and the seat of Monterey County.

John was the third of four children and the only son of Olive and John Ernst Steinbeck II. John's grandfather came from Germany, where the family name was Grossteinbeck. He was an adventurous man who traveled to Palestine as a missionary and later was drafted into the Confederate Army during the Civil War. He managed to escape and came to California, where he shortened his last name to Steinbeck to sound less foreign.

John's family was very close-knit, which helped them get through some tough times. His father struggled through one business disappointment after another, it seemed. First, he couldn't make a go of managing a flour mill. When he tried to run his own business by opening a feed store, it did not do well either. Because the Steinbecks were so well regarded within the community as hard-working, honest people, the local townspeople rallied behind them. A family friend got John's father an accounting job with a local sugar company. Then he was appointed Monterey County treasurer and held that job for the rest of his working life.

The job provided a steady income. While the family wasn't wealthy by any means, they lived comfortably enough. Young John had everything he desired, including a pony named Jill he shared with his little sister Mary, who was three years younger. His two older sisters, Esther and Beth, doted on him. Even though John enjoyed their company, he would often prefer to go off on his own. He spent countless days roaming the area around Salinas, which only had around 4,000 people living there at the time. He particularly loved the Monterey Peninsula. The Big Sur region with its majestic sea cliffs and its dark, misty forests enthralled him.

In his novel, *East of Eden,* Steinbeck would remember the effect of those surroundings. "I remember that the Gabilan Mountains to the east of the valley were light gay mountains, full of sun and loveliness and a kind of invitation, so that you wanted to climb into their warm foothills, almost as you wanted to climb into the lap of a beloved mother."[1] In *Travels with Charley,* he added, "I remember how once, in that part of youth that is deeply concerned with death, I wanted to be buried on this peak where without eyes I could see everything that I knew and loved, for in those days there was no world beyond the mountains."[2]

John was very close to his mother, Olive Hamilton Steinbeck shown below. She raised her four children to appreciate the arts, especially theater. Even so, Olive encouraged John to pursue a career in medicine. She wanted him in a profession that would give him financial security.

Chapter **2**   SURROUNDED BY NATURE

Both John's parents believed in exposing their children to the arts. They frequently took family trips to San Francisco to attend the theater. Olive, a former schoolteacher, was particularly keen on encouraging her son to read and instilling a love for the written word in him. When he was nine years old, his aunt gave him a book that absolutely mesmerized him. It was *Morte d'Arthur* (The Death of Arthur) by Sir Thomas Malory. The book, which recounts the legends of King Arthur and the Knights of the Round Table at Camelot, literally changed his life.

Years later, in the introduction to his book *The Acts of King Arthur and His Noble Knights*, Steinbeck wrote about the moral connection he felt to the tales of Lancelot and the search for the Holy Grail. "I think my sense of right and wrong, my feeling of *noblesse oblige* and any thought I may have against the oppressor and for the oppressed, came from this secret book,"[3] he explained. The book was more than just entertainment for John. It gave him a road map for social justice.

Despite her own love of literature, Olive didn't encourage her son to be a writer. Perhaps because of the bitter memories of doing without many things when her husband had been unable to keep a job, Olive hoped John would choose a career in medicine or law. But that was not meant to be. When he was fifteen, John announced he wanted to be a professional writer. His father supported him wholeheartedly while Olive could only worry and hope he would change his mind.

John attended Salinas High School but had little motivation to excel. He was more interested in developing his writing skills than in learning history or math. As a result of his single-mindedness, he was an indifferent student. He was also very self-conscious. Tall and gangly, he worried about his looks.

He hid his insecurities behind boisterous behavior that earned him the reputation of being a class clown. He became popular enough that he was elected class president. He was also the associate editor of his high school's yearbook, *El Gabilan*.

During the summers John began working in the fields, developing a love for the land and an appreciation and respect for the migrant workers who put in long, hot hours. John would cultivate the soil, fill and carry bags of grain at harvest time and work with cattle when the harvesting was finished. Through it all, he kept writing, his drawer filling with manuscripts.

Despite his determination, few people in Salinas considered John to be a special talent. During the summers of 1919 and 1920, John worked as an assistant to the chemist at the Spreckels sugar beet refinery. Rev. M. L. Kemper, former pastor of the First Presbyterian Church, said that John hardly seemed destined for greatness. "I was a few years older than John," Rev. Kemper recalled, "and when I left in the summer of 1920 to go to theological school, he took my job as night chemist. I wish I could tell you I saw something outstanding about him in those days, but I just remember him as an ordinary boy. It wasn't until the *Grapes of Wrath* was published that I even knew he was the same fellow I used to work with."[4]

After graduating from Salinas High School in 1919, John enrolled at Stanford University, mostly to appease his mother. He majored in English but wasn't particularly driven to earn a degree. Instead, he only took courses that interested him–primarily English composition and literature–and pursued a program of independent study. He was restless and found concentrating on academics difficult. Not even writing articles for *The Stanford Spectator* could hold his interest. Not surprisingly, he missed a lot of classes and withdrew in the autumn of his second year. He went to work on a ranch, where he spent his free time discussing politics with the other workers. Eventually he returned to college but found that very little had changed. All told, Steinbeck attended Stanford on and off for the next six years. But he never earned a college degree.

John might not have gained much by attending classes. He made up for that with his experiences out of school. In those years he met hoboes, factory workers, and migrant fruit pickers and always listened to their stories. The more his understanding of the human condition increased, the more his writing improved. Finally, someone saw his promise and challenged John to improve. Stanford English Professor Edith Ronald Mirrielees persuaded Steinbeck that he needed better discipline in order to succeed as a writer. That meant doing lots of revising because he often used lots of words to embellish his writing. Mirrielees encouraged him to keep his sentences shorter because they were more powerful that way.

Steinbeck dropped out of college for good in 1925. He was determined to make his living as a writer and decided it was time to leave California to try his fortunes back east. But he would find New York to be a chilly place indeed.

FYInfo

World's Fair

One of the cultural attractions that would have been a must-see for John and Olive Steinbeck was the 1915 World's Fair in San Francisco. Named the Panama Pacific International Exposition, the fair was both a celebration commemorating the completion of the Panama Canal as well as the 400th anniversary of the discovery of the Pacific Ocean by the explorer Vasco Nuñez de Balboa. It took three years to build the pavilions but the investment was worth it, particularly because the fair was a much-needed boost to the city which had been devastated nine years earlier by the infamous San Francisco earthquake and fire.

The exposition was held in the area now known as the Marina and covered an area of 635 acres. The most recognizable building was the Tower of Jewels, which stood over forty-three stories tall and was covered by more than a hundred thousand "jewels" of colored glass that reflected light in a dazzling display. Although most of the buildings were meant to be

The Panama Pacific
International Exposition

temporary, the Palace of Fine Arts was a permanent structure and was restored in the 1960s.

The fair attracted some of the most famous writers of the day, including poet Edwin Markham. According to the Exposition's website, Markham described the fair this way: "I have seen tonight the greatest revelation of beauty that was ever seen on this Earth. I may say this meaning it literally and with full regard for all that is known of ancient art and architecture and all that the modern world has heretofore seen of glory and grandeur. I have seen beauty that will give the world new standards of art, and a joy in loveliness never before reached."[1]

Steinbeck poses for a picture taken in the early 1930s. Although by this time his first book had been published he was still largely unknown. During this time he married Carol Henning. Together, they survived the Great Depression by growing their own food while living in the Steinbeck's family cottage.

Chapter 3

BREAKING THROUGH

Just as it still is today, Manhattan—one of the five boroughs that make up New York City—was the heart of the publishing business. Steinbeck hoped that mere proximity would improve his opportunities. Looking forward to an adventure, and to travel cheaply, Steinbeck got a job aboard a freight boat heading to New York via the Panama Canal. He decided to spend some time in Panama in order to absorb the local flavor but made the mistake of joining in a game of dice. He lost almost all his money and was basically penniless when he landed in New York.

He soon got a job as a hod carrier with the construction crew building Madison Square Garden. He had to wheel hundred-pound wheelbarrows of concrete along scaffolding that was suspended high above the streets of New York. It was difficult, dangerous work that sometimes lasted 15 to 18 hours a day.

Fortunately, he was eventually able to find a job as a newspaper reporter. Unfortunately, he was fired for adding too many personal opinions in the articles he wrote. Then he tried to make his living as a freelance writer, but he could not get anyone to publish his work.

Once again, Steinbeck was broke. Lack of sleep and lack of proper nutrition finally took its toll. He was also trying to get over a breakup with a young woman he had been dating. While walking down a New York street, John collapsed and had to be taken to the hospital. Once he had recuperated enough to travel, he swallowed his pride and worked his way back to California on another freighter.

The sting of having failed in New York was tempered by being back home in familiar surroundings. Steinbeck took a job as a caretaker of a large estate bordering on Lake Tahoe where he had worked previously. He rededicated himself to writing. Other than chopping wood and going to town once a week for supplies, John was able to spend the entire winter writing. During this time he wrote three novels; two were never submitted and the third was rejected by the publishers to whom he sent it.

In February 1928, he finished another book. It was *Cup of Gold*, an historical tale about an infamous 17th century Welsh pirate named Sir Henry Morgan. Finally his hard work paid off. The book was published in 1929. Although it wasn't a huge success, it gave self-confidence to the struggling writer. It also earned him enough money so that he could get married. While working at the estate he had met and fallen in love with Carol Henning. Their wedding came in 1930.

Steinbeck wrote two more novels in quick succession, *Pastures of Heaven* (1932) and *To a God Unknown* (1933). He received critical praise but little public recognition. By then the country was deep into the Great Depression. John felt its effect when his publisher went bankrupt, robbing him of what little earnings he had made on his books. John and Carol moved into the Steinbeck family cottage in Pacific Grove, which overlooks Monterey Bay. As his character in *Of Mice and Men* would say, they lived off the fat of the land. Supplemented by twenty-five dollars a month from his father, John put food on the table by catching fish and growing vegetables.

He kept writing, no matter how discouraging things got. Those days were professionally difficult but personally comforting as he, Carol, and a group of friends supported each other through the hard times. One was a marine biologist named Ed Ricketts, who would become John's closest friend. They enjoyed long talks, which helped John form many of his ideas more clearly.

"We pooled our troubles, our money when we had some, our inventiveness and our pleasures," he wrote many years later. "I remember it as a warm and friendly time. Only illness frightened us. You have to have money to be sick, with the result that my teeth went badly to pieces. Without dough you couldn't have a tooth filled. Keeping clean was also a problem because soap cost money. For a time we washed our laundry with a soap made of pork fat, wood ashes and salt. It worked, but it took a lot of sunning to get the smell out of the sheets."[1]

Selling stories and books was particularly challenging. "Even if they had been good, they would have come back because publishers were hardest hit of all," he explained. When people are broke, the first things they give up are books. I couldn't even afford postage on the manuscripts. It's not easy to go on writing constantly with little hope that anything will come of it. But I do remember it as a time of warmth and mutual caring. If one of us got hurt or ill or in trouble the others rallied with what they had. Everyone shared bad fortune as well as good."[2]

Chapter **3**   BREAKING THROUGH

Steinbeck's fortune was about to change. Back in New York, a publisher named Pascal Covici bought a copy of *Pastures of Heaven* to read while on a train trip. He was so impressed with the writing that he immediately tracked down Steinbeck to see if he had written anything else. As fate would have it, John was currently sending a book around. Seven publishers had already turned it down. Covici asked to read it. The book was *Tortilla Flat*. It was about to put Steinbeck on the literary, and public, map.

Since moving into his parent's three-room cottage, Steinbeck had gotten into the habit of wandering up to the *paisano* settlement above the town of Monterey. He passed many an afternoon drinking wine and talking to the *paisanos*, or Americans of Mexican descent, many of whom he had first met as a kid. It was from these experiences that Steinbeck got the inspiration for *Tortilla Flat*, an often humorous but always sympathetic look at the lives of *paisanos* and others living in Monterey. The hero of the book, Danny, was modeled after a well-known local fisherman named Benny. The book itself had resemblances to *Morte d'Arthur*, with Danny showing some of the same characteristics as King Arthur.

Tortilla Flat was a critical *and* popular success. John would win the California Commonwealth Club's Gold Medal for the best novel by a California author that year. A Hollywood studio paid him $4,000 for the film rights. After the book went into seven printings the first year, Covici signed Steinbeck for his next six books.

But John's success was bittersweet. His mother Olive had died in 1934, after John had gone home to help care for her. His father died a year later. It would be one of his life's biggest regrets that his parents did not live to see him succeed as a writer.

FYInfo

Ed Ricketts

One of Monterey's most famous citizens was marine biologist Ed Ricketts. He came to Monterey from Chicago in 1923 and opened the Pacific Biological Laboratories, which supplied biological specimens and slides to schools and research institutions.

When Steinbeck met Ed seven years later, the two men became immediate friends. Ricketts had a profound influence on John's writing–so much so that he became the inspiration for the character Doc in the books *Cannery Row* and *Sweet Thursday* as well as several other works. In 1940, Ricketts and Steinbeck spent a month on a boat in the Gulf of California collecting marine life specimens. That resulted in the book *The Sea of Cortez,* which both men co-authored.

Ricketts never let his celebrity status, nor his friendship with Steinbeck, distract him from his work. Stanford University published his ecological handbook on marine life, *Between Pacific Tides,* in 1939. Now in its fifth edition, the work is still used as a textbook at many universities.

After Steinbeck moved to New York during World War II, he and Ricketts fell out of touch. The two had plans to take another collecting

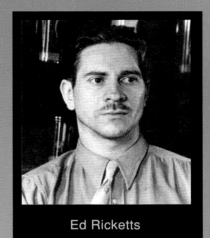

Ed Ricketts

trip to the Queen Charlotte Islands off the coast of British Columbia. They never got the chance. A train struck Ricketts's car on May 8, 1948 and he died three days later.

His legacy continues. A sea spider originally collected by Ricketts was named *Pycnogonum rickettsi* after him. A collection of his scientific and philosophical essays, *The Outer Shores,* was published in 1978. Moss Landing Marine Laboratory christened their research vessel the *RV Ed Ricketts* the following year. In 1994, the City of Pacific Grove renamed High Street, where his first lab once stood, as Ricketts Row. After Ed's original Pacific Biological Laboratory was closed, it later became a gathering place for the artists and musicians who founded the first Monterey Jazz Festival, one of the country's leading music festivals.

By the late 1930s, Steinbeck was regarded as one of America's most important writers. The novels *Tortilla Flat* and *Of Mice and Men* also made him famous the world over. Success meant he and Carol could afford their own home. Now that he didn't have to worry as much about money, Steinbeck was able to concentrate fully on writing.

Chapter 4

GIVING WORKERS A VOICE

It wasn't until after *Tortilla Flat* was published that Steinbeck realized just how much of a toll the death of his parents and the strain of struggling to make it had taken on him. He was exhausted and knew he needed to recharge his creative energies. As soon as he received some royalties from *Tortilla Flat*, Steinbeck took a three-month trip to Mexico with Carol. It was also an attempt to repair his relationship with her, as she had begun to feel neglected. Steinbeck was so focused on his writing and with gathering ideas that he and Carol had grown apart. The couple enjoyed their time in Mexico. Steinbeck had no way of knowing that it would be one of the last times he would be able to travel anonymously. By the time they returned to California, he learned that *Tortilla Flat* had become a hit. Suddenly, John Steinbeck was a success.

Now that he was a respected literary figure, the stories poured out of him. His next book was

In Dubious Battle, a bitterly realistic political novel about a labor strike by California fruit pickers. It was a subject close to his heart. Growing up in Salinas, Steinbeck had witnessed first-hand the exploitation of farm workers. He channeled his rage over the injustice onto the pages of his book. He based the story on a strike that had taken place in the fruit-growing section of Watsonville, a community twenty miles from Salinas. However, John refused to take sides in the book. He wrote a story that included the points of view of both laborers and growers. It was so balanced that both political conservatives and liberals took issue with him.

Although neither critics nor the public warmed to *In Dubious Battle*, it still managed to further Steinbeck's reputation, in one way or another. The Commonwealth Club of San Francisco appreciated the book's insight into the troublesome labor question. They gave John their gold medal, which is awarded annually to the best novel written by a Californian. At the same time, however, a committee of citizens demanded that all of Steinbeck's books be removed from the shelves of the local library.

John and Carol decided to take a break from Monterey. They moved to Los Gatos, a tranquil community an hour outside San Francisco. They built a house and put a fence around it with a gate that could be locked to ensure their privacy. As soon as they were settled, John resumed writing at a furious pace. He got up at dawn every morning to write at his oak desk in his small workroom. As he approached the end of a book, he would grow impatient and excited, pressing to the finish and sleeping in the same room as the manuscript.

He almost called his next book *Something That Happened* and actually toyed with the idea of it being a children's book.

Soon disaster struck. His puppy Toby ate more than half the manuscript. It was the only copy. In those days, of course, there weren't computers that saved work. John lost two months of work and had to rewrite everything that had been eaten.

That book, ultimately named *Of Mice and Men*, was chosen by the Book of the Month Club, guaranteeing it a large audience and big sales. It leapt to the top of the best-seller lists when it was released. John was taken aback, calling the news "gratifying but also frightening."[1] In its first month of publication, the book sold more than 117,000 copies, prompting Steinbeck to observe, "That's a hell of a lot of books."[2] Suddenly, John Steinbeck was famous. And it made him uncomfortable, in part because like many people who lived through the Great Depression, he feared having everything taken away from him again.

Many years later, he admitted, "My books were beginning to sell better than I had ever hoped or expected and while this was pleasing it also frightened me. I knew it couldn't last and I was afraid my standard of living would go up and leave me stranded when the next collapse came. We were much more accustomed to collapse than to prosperity. Also I had an archaic angry-gods feeling that made me give a great lot of my earnings away. I was a pushover for anyone or any organization asking for money. I guess it was a kind of propitiation. It didn't make sense that a book, a humble, hat-in-hand, rejected book, was now eagerly bought—even begged for. I didn't trust it. But I did begin to get around more."[3]

Of Mice and Men was the story of two migrant farm hands, one of them borderline retarded. They dream of being able to settle on their own plot of land but only find tragedy because of their association with the flirtatious wife of the landowner.

Steinbeck had actually conceived this story as a play in novella form, so he was able to easily adapt it for the stage. It struck just as intense a chord with theatergoers as it had with readers. The play was a Broadway hit and went on to be made into a movie.

In *Of Mice and Men*, Steinbeck had finally been able to successfully marry good story telling within the context of a social cause—in this case, the plight of migrant workers. Art usually imitates life. Perhaps now art could actually help change life. Fame had given Steinbeck a platform to express his views and he took advantage of it. *The San Francisco News* hired him to write a series of articles called "The Harvest Gypsies" on the conditions of migrant labor in Southern California. In one of the articles, Steinbeck argued, "Agricultural workers should be encouraged and helped to organize...The same arguments are used against the organizing of agricultural labor as were used against the organizing of the craft and skilled labor unions. It was argued then that industry could not survive if labor were organized. It is argued today that agriculture cannot exist if farm labor is organized. It is reasonable to believe that agriculture would suffer no more from organization than industry has."[4]

In 1938, John published two books. One was a collection of short stories called *The Long Valley*. The other was *Their Blood is Strong*, a compilation of his "Harvest Gypsies" articles.

All these books were just leading up to what is widely considered to be Steinbeck's masterpiece.

When *The Grapes of Wrath* was published in 1939, it created a literary explosion not just in the United States but also around the world. The book told the story of the Joad family, poor Oklahoma farmers who travel to the Promised Land of

California during the Depression in search of hope. They can only find salvation through terrible suffering. The Biblical themes were quite intentional. They harkened back to the same kind of moral code that Steinbeck had found so

The Great Depression saw millions of people out of work. People everywhere lost their homes. After a terrible drought hit the Midwest, millions of farmers moved to California to look for work. These migrant workers and the harsh lives they led would be the inspiration for Steinbeck's masterpiece, *The Grapes of Wrath*.

compelling in *Morte d'Arthur.* In many ways, it was a book he had been researching his entire life.

The Grapes of Wrath won Steinbeck the Pulitzer Prize as the best novel of the year as well as the American Bookseller's Award and membership in the National Institute of Arts and Letters. The political impact of the book was so great that President Franklin D. Roosevelt met with Steinbeck.

But he also faced a severe backlash. The novel was virtually banned in Oklahoma. Landowners in California resented their depiction as exploiters of the downtrodden. The book was so controversial that at one point Steinbeck actually worried about his safety.

"The vilification of me out here from the large landowners and bankers is pretty bad," he wrote. "The latest is a rumor started by them that the Okies hate me and have threatened to kill me for lying about them. I'm frightened at the rolling might of this damned thing. It is completely out of hand. I mean a kind of hysteria about the book is growing that is not healthy."[5]

It's sobering to note that over sixty years later, both *Of Mice and Men* and *The Grapes of Wrath* are still often found on lists of commonly banned books.

Steinbeck dealt with the controversy and the worst of it soon passed. However, he was having a much more difficult time learning to be a public figure, a battle he would wage the rest of his life. His desire to have some time away from celebrity would cause a major shift in the direction his next books would take.

FYInfo

Hollywood

Hollywood has always loved a good story. From its earliest days, movie studios used the work of top writers. In turn, high-profile authors like Steinbeck knew a successful movie made from one of their novels might mean increased book sales.

While all kinds of books have been made into movies, those with political themes were particularly sought after. Some of the most successful films during the time of Steinbeck's early career tackled social and political issues. In the 1930s and 1940s, films such as *Mr. Smith Goes to Washington* and *Meet John Doe,* both directed by Frank Capra, portrayed men fighting for the rights of the common man. This was a theme that resonated with the United States coming out of a devastating depression. The idealistic tone and upbeat endings of these movies were meant to inspire hope in the American public.

Possibly the most famous political movie is *All the King's Men*. It is based on Robert Penn Warren's novel, which won the Pulitzer Prize for Literature in 1947. The movie won an Oscar for Best Picture in 1949.

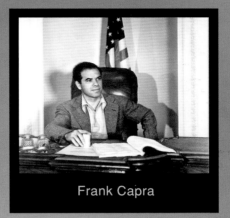

Frank Capra

There were probably more movies made in the 1930s and 1940s that dealt with controversial issues than in recent years. At that time budgets for movies were small and many more movies were made. Because films cost so much to produce today, studios are hesitant to make a movie that might offend anyone. It's rare to find a film that takes a political stand the way *Of Mice and Men* did in 1939 and *The Grapes of Wrath* a year later.

Although it did not win an Oscar, the film adaptation of *The Grapes of Wrath*, directed by John Ford and starring Henry Fonda as Tom Joad, was named one of the best movies of the past 100 years by the American Picture Association. Screen adaptations of Steinbeck's works have won four Awards and received a total of 29 Academy Award nominations.

In 1962, Steinbeck was awarded the Nobel Prize in Literature. In his acceptance speech he talked about the responsibility of being a writer. "The ancient commission of the writer has not changed. He is charged with exposing our many grievous faults and failures, with dredging up to light our dark and dangerous dreams for the purpose of improvement."

Chapter 5

A LITERARY LEGACY

For Steinbeck, being a famous author was just as emotionally difficult as it had been being a struggling writer. He quickly learned that success and celebrity simply meant giving up one set of problems for another. On one hand, life was easier because he had more money and didn't have to worry about buying food. On the other, the social requirements of fame wore him down and depleted his spirit. He preferred living simply and he hated literary parties filled with pretentious people trying to impress one another. His shyness made invitations to be a guest speaker or having to sign autographs anxiety-filled moments. The truth was that he still felt most at home with the ordinary people he chose to write about: the farmers, fruit pickers and factory workers.

Steinbeck's ambivalence about fame and his generosity were reflected in subtle ways. When he won the Pulitzer Prize in 1940 for *The Grapes of Wrath*, he gave the award money to a newspaper in Pacific Grove, sharing food and resources with all his struggling friends. But there was a difference. Steinbeck might have felt he was the same person with or without money. But people began to treat him differently, either because he was now famous or because they took issue with his novels. Either way, he found he wasn't as welcome anymore.

The pain this caused him is evident in a letter he wrote years later. "Don't think for a moment that you will ever be forgiven for being what they call 'different.' You won't! I still have not been forgiven. Only when I am delivered in a pine box will I be considered 'safe.' After I had written the *Grapes of Wrath* and it had been to a large extent read and sometimes burned, the librarians at the Salinas Public Library, who had known my folks remarked that is was lucky my parents were dead so that they did not have to suffer this shame."[1]

So after the hoopla surrounding *The Grapes of Wrath*, which was on its way to selling more than half a million copies, Steinbeck announced he needed a long vacation. In 1940, he escaped with his best friend Ed Ricketts on an adventure that rejuvenated him. He accompanied Ed on a biological expedition to collect marine samples along the northern coast of California. The experience was so exhilarating for Steinbeck that he joined Ricketts on a second expedition, this time to the south, a trip he would later recount in his book *The Sea of Cortez*. Soon after that, Steinbeck traveled to Mexico to work on a documentary film, *The Forgotten Village*. While all the travel may have energized John, it also tore apart his marriage. Carol, who often had remained behind in Pacific Grove while her husband took trip after trip, finally had enough and filed for divorce in 1942.

A year after splitting with Carol, John married a singer named Gwyndolyn Conger. She was nearly twenty years younger than Steinbeck. Despite the major part his traveling had played in the breakup of his first marriage, John seemed unable to stay settled. Shortly after marrying Gwyn, he went on a four-month assignment as a war correspondent. When he finally returned, he settled down long enough in the couple's new home in New York to have two children, Thom and John. But Gwyn resented that John was more attentive to his writing than he was to his wife and children.

In 1945, Steinbeck published *Cannery Row*. Unlike his previous novels, this one was not at all political. Instead it was an homage to the people he had met in Monterey, including Ed Ricketts, who Steinbeck immortalized as the character "Doc." Steinbeck would later explain he had written *Cannery Row* as a sort of therapy. After seeing so much horror on the battlefield, he wanted to return to the area, the times, and the people he had loved so much as a young, struggling writer. Though the novel was not very successful, Hollywood came calling again and snapped up the movie rights. When his next novel, *The Wayward Bus*, also failed to generate many sales in 1947, Steinbeck turned his attention to writing motion-picture scripts.

But John's life would soon take an abrupt and unexpected turn. In 1948, Steinbeck got the news that Ed Ricketts had been killed. Stunned, he flew to California for the funeral. When he returned back east, Gwyn told him she had filed for divorce. Within a matter of days, John's world had completely turned upside down. He suddenly found himself without his best friend, without a wife and in debt. Although he had some royalties from earlier works, Steinbeck owed alimony, child support, and taxes. Depressed, broke and seeking the comfort of familiar surroundings and old friends, Steinbeck retreated to the cottage in Pacific Grove. He was so strapped for cash he had to ask his publisher, Pat Covici, to send him writing paper. As usual, his writing saved him.

Longing for happier times, John immersed himself in the California of his youth. He wandered through all his old hangouts and spent countless hours at the library researching old newspaper articles. As news spread among the locals that Steinbeck was back and was working on a new book, many of them viewed him with distrust. The resentment caused by *The Grapes of Wrath* still lingered almost a decade later. As Steinbeck noted, "I am told that a little quiver of terror has crept through old Salinas at the project. I am on no punitive expedition. I just want it straight."[2]

He went on to observe that people had started telling tall tales about him, including "the throwing of the roast of beef through the glass door at City Hall. I have become a giant kind of half criminal, half ape over there. I have a whole life and adventures in Salinas all of which are new to me."[3]

But John was not dissuaded. "I am on my marathon book, which is called *Salinas Valley*. It is what I have been practicing to write all of my life. Everything else has been training."[4]

While researching his new book, Steinbeck met Elaine Scott. Many people believe that she was the true love of his life. Elaine was able to get John out of his shell and find joy in life again. She was also able to ease him back into social settings that had previously caused him so much anxiety. They were married in 1950. Because neither John's old friends nor Monterey were the way he remembered them, or needed them to be, the couple moved back to New York. Steinbeck would spend the rest of his life there.

The book he spent years working on would eventually be published in 1952 as *East of Eden*. It spans the period from the American Civil War to World War I and reveals the history of the Salinas Valley through the story of two families who find new lives there. Steinbeck would later say he considered it the best book of his career. It also became a successful movie starring James Dean.

Though Steinbeck continued to write, most of his output for the rest of the decade was not well received by critics. Some of them even suggested that perhaps Steinbeck's time had come—and gone. But he soon proved them wrong.

In 1961, Steinbeck made a literary comeback with the publication of *The Winter of Our Discontent*, the story of a man from a distinguished New England family who betrays his idealism through fear of insecurity. The book mirrored Steinbeck's worry over the moral corruption he believed was growing in America. Once again, Steinbeck had a critical and popular success on his hands. Once again, he felt restless.

Rather than just enjoy his comeback, Steinbeck decided that he had become too comfortable. Against the warnings of his doctors, who worried about his ill health, John took off on a 10,000-mile cross country trip. His only companion was his poodle, Charley. Steinbeck said he wanted to rediscover America. The journal he kept was published as *Travels With Charley*. In it he wrote, "I knew that ten or twelve thousand miles driving a truck, alone and unattended, over every kind of road, would be hard work, but to me it represented the antidote for the poison of the professional sick man. And in my own life I am not willing to trade quality for quantity. If this

39

projected journey should prove too much, then it was time to go anyway. I see too many men delay their exits with a sickly, slow reluctance to leave the stage. It's bad theater as well as bad living."[5]

There was no longer any question that Steinbeck was one of the great literary figures, not just in the United States, but in the entire world. It was only fitting that the judges of the Swedish Academy honored Steinbeck with the world-famous Nobel Prize for Literature in 1962. From that point on, however, Steinbeck never published another novel. He spent his time writing articles. In early 1966, he even traveled to Vietnam as a war correspondent for the New York newspaper, *Newsday*.

But he was forced to finally slow down the following year when his health began to fail. He suffered a series of strokes and on December 20, 1968, he died of a heart attack at the age of 66 with Elaine by his side.

There was never a question of where Steinbeck would be buried. Elaine and his son Thom had John's ashes interred in his family's cemetery plot back in Salinas, California.

Early in his career, Steinbeck had once written his friend George Albee, "I think I would like to write the story of this whole valley, of all the little towns and all the farms and the ranches in the wilder hills. I can see how I would like to do it so that it would be the valley of the world."[6]

Through the legacy of his work, Steinbeck accomplished that, and much more.

FYInfo

1962

American society was still very politically and culturally conservative in 1962, the year that Steinbeck won his Nobel Prize. Women were expected to be stay-at-home mothers, divorce was a scandal and children were warned against arguing with their elders. Just a few years later, with the cultural revolution of 1968 spurred by the war in Vietnam, that would all change. A good way to get a sense of what else was happening in the world while Steinbeck was being honored is to take a look at the entertainment that was popular at the time and other accomplishments that were being recognized.

Other Nobel Prizes of Note: Francis Crick and James Watson, along with Maurice Wilkins, won in the Physiology and Medicine category for discovering the double helix structure of DNA.

Linus Pauling, who had won the Nobel Prize in Chemistry in 1954 and later became best known for promoting the beneficial effects of Vitamin C against colds, was awarded the Nobel Peace Prize for his efforts in promoting nuclear disarmament.

Pulitzer Prize for Literature
Edwin O'Connor, *The Edge of Sadness*

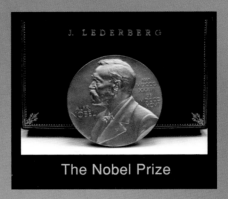

The Nobel Prize

The Academy Awards
Best Picture: *Lawrence of Arabia*
Best Actor: Gregory Peck, *To Kill a Mockingbird*
Best Actress: Anne Bancroft, *The Miracle Worker*

Grammy Awards
Best New Artist: Robert Goulet
Album of the Year: *The First Family*, Vaughn Meader
Record of the Year: *I Left My Heart in San Francisco,* Tony Bennett
Best Performance by a Vocal Group: *If I Had a Hammer*, Peter, Paul & Mary

Emmys
Outstanding Drama: *The Defenders*
Best Actor in a Series Lead: E.G. Marshall, *The Defenders*
Best Actress in a Series Lead: Shirley Booth, *Hazel*
Outstanding supporting actor: Don Knotts, *The Andy Griffith Show*
Outstanding Performance in a Variety Series: Carol Burnett

CHRONOLOGY

1902 Born on February 27 in Salinas, California

1911 Receives copy of *Morte d'Arthur* as a birthday present

1916 Declares intention to become a writer

1919 Enters Stanford University

1925 Quits college and travels to New York, where he remains for several months before returning to California

1929 Publishes first novel, *Cup of Gold*

1930 Marries Carol Henning; meets Edward F. Ricketts, who becomes lifelong friend

1934 Spends winter investigating farm labor unions

1935 Scores first popular success with publication of novel *Tortilla Flat*

1937 Publishes *Of Mice and Men*; the stage version opens on Broadway and earns the New York Drama Critics Award

1938 Writes *Their Blood Is Strong*, a nonfiction account of the migrant labor problem in California

1939 Publishes *The Grapes of Wrath,* a popular and critical success

1940 Receives the National Book Award and the Pulitzer Prize for *The Grapes of Wrath*

1942 Divorces Carol

1943 Marries Gwyn Conger in New Orleans; is hired as a war correspondent by the *New York Herald Tribune*

1944 First child, Thom, is born

1945 Publishes *Cannery Row*

1946 Second son, John IV, is born; receives Norway's King Haakon Liberty Cross

1948 Divorces Gwyn; is elected to American Academy of Arts and Letters

1950 Marries third wife, Elaine Anderson Scott

1952 Publishes *East of Eden*

1961 Publishes *The Winter of Our Discontent*, his twelfth novel

1962 Awarded the Nobel Prize for Literature

1964 Presented United States Medal of Freedom by President Lyndon B. Johnson

1968 Dies of arteriosclerosis on December 20 in New York

1979 U.S. Postal Service issues a commemorative stamp on what would have been his 77th birthday

TIMELINE IN HISTORY

1850	California is admitted to the Union as the 31st state.
1861	The U.S. Civil War begins; it ends four years later.
1871	Stephen Crane, the author of *The Red Badge of Courage*, is born.
1876	Alexander Graham Bell invents the telephone.
1889	William Dickson, working with Thomas Edison, builds first motion camera and calls it the Kinetograph.
1896	The first modern Olympic Games are held in Athens, Greece.
1902	Beatrix Potter publishes *The Tale of Peter Rabbit*.
1906	An earthquake devastates San Francisco.
1908	Henry Ford introduces the Model-T.
1913	Ford introduces the movable assembly line.
1916	Jack London, author of *Call of the Wild*, dies at the age of 40.
1927	Union leader César Chavez is born in Yuma, Arizona.
1929	The U.S. stock market crashes on October 29, marking the beginning of the Great Depression.
1936	Bert Corona begins to organize unions for cannery and warehouse workers in California.
1938	On assignment for *The Light* newspaper, singer/social activist Woody Guthrie investigates conditions of migrant workers.
1941	Pearl Harbor is bombed; America enters World War II.
1945	World War II ends.
1950	The Korean War begins; it ends three years later.
1962	César Chavez establishes the National Farm Workers Association; author William Faulkner dies.
1968	Civil rights leader Dr. Martin Luther King and presidential candidate Robert F. Kennedy are assassinated.
1969	Neil Armstrong becomes first man to step on the moon in July; the Woodstock music festival takes place in August.
1974	President Richard Nixon resigns from office.
1976	Alex Haley publishes *Root,* the story of several generations of African Americans.
1981	Sandra Day O'Connor is appointed first female U.S. Supreme Court Justice.
1986	Dr. Franklin R. Chang-Diaz becomes the first Hispanic-American astronaut as he takes off in the space shuttle *Columbia*.
1989	An earthquake of magnitude 7.1 hits the San Francisco Bay area.
1991	Tim Berners-Lee introduces the first website on the internet.
1996	At the age of 16, tennis player Martina Hingis becomes the youngest Wimbledon champion in history as she wins the women's doubles.
2003	Arnold Schwarzenegger is elected governor of California.
2004	Former U.S. President Bill Clinton's autobiography *My Life* sells more than one million copies in the first eight days of it's publication.

CHAPTER NOTES

Chapter 1
An Eye For Detail
1. Marco R. della Cava, "In Search of John Steinbeck." USA TODAY, April 8, 2002.
2. www.nobel.se/literature/laureates/1962
3. Ibid.
4. Ibid.

Chapter 2
Surrounded by Nature
1. John Steinbeck, *East of Eden* (New York: Penguin, 2002), p. 3.
2. John Steinbeck, *Travels with Charley* (New York: Penguin, 1997), p. 157.
3. John Steinbeck, *The Acts of King Arthur and His Noble Knights* (New York: Noonday Press, 1993), p. 3.
4. Charles E. Claffey, "Salinas makes its peace with Steinbeck, a native son," *Boston Globe,* 13 August 1981.
FYI: World's Fair
1. www.sanfranciscomemories.com/ppie/panamapacific.html

Chapter 3
Breaking Through
1. John Steinbeck, "I Remember the Thirties," *Esquire,* June 1960.
2. Ibid.

Chapter 4
Giving Workers a Voice
1. Jay Parini, *John Steinbeck: A Biography* (New York: Henry Holt, 1995), p. 182.
2. Ibid., p. 183.
3. John Steinbeck, "I Remember the Thirties," *Esquire,* June 1960.
4. John Steinbeck, "The Harvest Gypsies," *San Francisco News*, 12 October 1936.
5. http://www.steinbeck.org/SSalinas.html

Chapter 5
A Literary Legacy
1. www.steinbeck.org/MainFrame.html
2. Ibid.
3. Ibid.
4. Ibid.
5. John Steinbeck, *Travels with Charley* (New York: Penguin, 1997), pp. 17-18.
6. Jay Parini, *John Steinbeck: A Biography* (New York: Henry Holt, 1995), p. 135.

FURTHER READING

For Young Adults

Bloom, Harold (ed.) and Ellyn Sanna and Michael Price. *John Steinbeck*. Broomall, Pennsylvania: Chelsea House Publishers, 2003.

Florence, Donne. *John Steinbeck: America's Author*. Berkeley Heights, N.J.: Enslow Publishers, 2000.

Reef, Catherine. *John Steinbeck*. Boston: Clarion Books, 2004.

Stanley, Jerry. *Children of the Dust Bowl: The True Story of the School at Weedpatch Camp*. New York: Crown Books for Young Readers, 1993.

Steinbeck, John. *The Pearl*. New York: Penguin USA, 2000.

Tessitore, John. *John Steinbeck: A Writer's Life*. New York: Franklin Watts, 2001.

Works Consulted

Astro, Richard. *John Steinbeck and Edward F. Ricketts: The Shaping of a Novelist*. Minneapolis: University of Minnesota Press, 1973.

Beck, Warren. "On John Steinbeck." *Talks With Authors*, pp. 56-72. Charles F. Madden, editor. Carbondale, Illinois: Southern Illinois University Press, 1968.

Benson, Jackson J. *The True Adventures of John Steinbeck, Writer*. New York: Viking, 1984.

Enea, Sparky. *With Steinbeck in the Sea of Cortez*. Los Osos, California: Sand River Press, 1991.

Fensch, Thomas. *Conversations with John Steinbeck*. Jackson, Mississippi: University Press of Mississippi, 1988.

Parini, Jay. *John Steinbeck: A Biography*. New York: Henry Holt, 1995.

Scully, Frank. *Rogue's Gallery: Profiles of My Eminent Contemporaries*. Hollywood, California: Murray and Gee, 1943.

Steinbeck, Elaine and Robert Walsten (editors). *Steinbeck, A Life in Letters*. New York: Viking, 1975.

Steinbeck, John. *The Acts of King Arthur and His Noble Knights*. New York: Noonday Press, 1993.

Steinbeck, John. *East of Eden*. New York: Penguin, 2002.

Steinbeck, John. "I Remember the Thirties." *Esquire*, June, 1960.

Steinbeck, John. *Travels with Charley*. New York: Penguin, 1997.

Steinbeck, John IV and Nancy Steinbeck and Andrew Harvey. *The Other Side of Eden: Life With John Steinbeck*. Amherst, New York: Prometheus Books, 2001.

Swisher, Clarice (ed.). *Readings on The Red Pony*. San Diego: Greenhaven Press, 2002.

FURTHER READING

On the Internet

The Nobel Prize in Literature 1962
  http://www.nobel.se/literature/laureates/1962/

Excerpts from Distinguished American Series: John Steinbeck
  http://www.lnu.edu.cn/englishw/novel/a12e.html

National Steinbeck Center
  http://www.steinbeck.org/MainFrame.html

Steinbeck and Salinas
  http://www.steinbeck.org/SSalinas.html

Monterey County Historical Society: John Steinbeck
  http://users.dedot.com/mchs/steinbeck.html

John Steinbeck Page
  http://ocean.st.usm.edu/~wsimkins/steinb.html

The Nobel Prize in Literature 1962
  http://www.nobel.se/literature/laureates/1962/

Sir Thomas Malory: Muse and Mentor for John Steinbeck
  http://www.arbutus.net/reviews/steinbeck.htm

From "The Harvest Gypsies"
  http://ocean.st.usm.edu/~wsimkins/gypsies.html

GLOSSARY

cannery (CAN-uhr-ee)
factory where farm products are
cleaned, separated and put into cans
drought (DRAWT)
period of abnormally dry weather
Dust Bowl
Great Plains region hardest hit by
the drought and windstorms during
the early 1930s
Great Depression (GRATE dee-PRESH-un)
worldwide economic slump that
began in the United States following
the Wall Street crash of October
1929 and eventually put hundreds of
millions of people out of work
hod (HAWD)
portable trough for carrying plaster,
mortar and bricks, fixed crosswise on
top of a pole and carried on a
person's shoulder
journalist (JUR-nahl-ist)
writer who tells stories about real
people and events, usually for a
newspaper or magazine
marine biologist (MUH-reen bye-AWL-oh-jist)
scientist who studies living creatures
in oceans, seas, bays, and other large
bodies of water
migrant worker (MY-grunt WERE-ker)
person who travels from one area to
another in search of work; usually
applied to agricultural workers

noblesse oblige (no-BLESS uh-BLIJE)
obligation to behave responsibly
associated with high rank
Okies (OH-kees)
farmers and other victims of the
Great Plains drought who headed to
California in search of migrant work
pavilion (puh-VILL-ee-uhn)
ornamental structure in an open
space, terrace or garden, with a roof
that is generally supported by pillars
propitiation (pro-PISH-ee-ay-shun)
to gain or regain the favor or good-
will of ; to give someone what they
want to make them happy
union (YOON-yun)
organization of workers overseeing
wages, benefits, and working conditions
valley (VAL-lee)
a low-lying area of land located
between hills or mountains
vilification (vil-ih-fuh-KAY-shun)
to speak of someone as if they
were a bad person

INDEX